Contents

About the author

Lorenza Clifford is founder of **Coachange Ltd**, a
company that provides top quality coaching to
individuals.

Career coaching helps people to find better balance in their
lives, to make their work enlivening and their leisure time
happier. We prepare our clients to rise to life's challenges
and to make the most of every opportunity.

Coachange Ltd works with clients from all walks of life
finding new ways to make quality coaching affordable.
We believe coaching can offer powerful help to ordinary
people, not just the elite.

Lorenza has a Masters degree in Occupational Psychology,
a coaching qualification and over a decade of experience
coaching blue chip clients at all levels of the organisation.
She is a member of the Association for Coaching and is
available for workshops, coaching, speaking, and writing.
To contact her, e-mail headoffice@coachange.co.uk or
telephone 01264 334897.

Visit her website at: **www.coachange.co.uk**

Thanks
My thanks go to Fiona Parashar of Leadership Coaching Ltd
for answering my questions and to Peter Ward who led me
to writing a long time ago. Thanks also to my editor, Lisa
Carden, and my family for all their support.

What type of interviewer are you?

Interviews can be as stressful for the interviewer as they are for the candidate — especially if they've not prepared properly! Answer the following questions, then read the guidance points for advice on how to make life easier for yourself.

1. How you do prepare to interview someone?
a) I don't, really. I just wing it.
b) I read all CVs and covering letters thoroughly.
c) I make up a different set of questions for each candidate.

2. Why is consistency important in interview questions?
a) Is it?
b) It means that everyone is measured fairly.
c) I think creativity is more important. I don't want to bore myself.

3. What do you look for in a candidate?
a) Someone just like me.
b) Someone with lots of potential, who fits closely to the person specification.
c) Someone who ticks every box in the person specification.

4. What is the best way to deal with a nervous candidate?

a) I tend to look at my watch a lot. They usually speed up.
b) I try to be reassuring and use positive body language to show I'm interested in what they're saying.
c) I tend to say nothing and let them think in silence.

5. What is the best way to deal with a chatty candidate?

a) I explain the next candidate is arriving in five minutes.
b) I find it quite hard. Normally I wait for a break in the conversation and then move on.
c) I normally interrupt and move the conversation on.

6. Where do you hold meetings?

a) In my office. It means that colleagues can come and interrupt if they need to.
b) I book a meeting room or use my office but close the door and turn off the phone.
c) In the boardroom. It's useful to see how candidates react to stress.

7. What type of questions must be avoided in interviews?

a) None! People need to be able to stand up for themselves.
b) Anything that could be seen as discriminatory, whether about race, religion, sexual preferences, or age.
c) I'm not sure.

a = 1, b = 2, c = 3.
Now add up your scores.

- **7–10**: You may be inadvertently terrifying candidates with your no-nonsense manner! Take a step back and think through the whole process to find out how improving your interpersonal skills can really make a difference. Chapter **3** is especially helpful on how to get things off to a good start. It's also essential that you find out more about questions that are unlawful in interviews. Chapter **3** can help here too.

- **11–17**: You have a pretty good handle on how to get the best from others at interview. Don't forget that you can be assertive if you need to to keep things on track and on time. Chapters **3** to **6** can help you boost your skills, whatever type of interview you're involved in

- **18–21**: You seem to be a mix of vagueness and abrasiveness. You mean well at points, but you really need to brush up on your people skills. As above, read Chapter **3** thoroughly to get yourself back on track. Putting some more time into preparation can really help too. Turn to Chapter **2** for advice on this.

Interviewing others:
The basics

Interviews are far and away the most common way of recruiting people. Nearly all organisations use interviews and they are conducted across the whole spectrum of jobs.

Their popularity aside, interviews are time-consuming: it has been estimated that they take up roughly two staff days per vacancy. This makes them expensive, with about 70% of companies paying all travel expenses, on top of employees' time, agency fees, and administrative costs. Perhaps because of the costs involved, the interview has been studied for more than 80 years. This research has led to specific recommendations on how to improve an interview's effectiveness for selection and how to improve decision-making based on it.

In this chapter we examine why the interview is a useful tool, what you can expect to get from it, and how it should be used. We also look at the common pitfalls that many interviewers encounter and how to avoid them.

Step one: Understand the overall place of interviews in selection

The aims of the selection process are to select and rank the applicants who:

- have the *ability* to perform the job well without suffering undue stress
- are *motivated* to work well in this position
- will *enhance the team* involved
- will improve the *organisation's likelihood of success* in the future

Interviewers can meet these aims by:

- making sure that the content of the interview is focused on a few critical factors that have been shown to link directly to successful job performance
- using interviews alongside other systematic selection processes, such as ability tests, to gather further information about the suitability of candidates
- choosing questions that will get participants to discuss their performance in situations similar to those they will face if they get the job
- using these questions to collect the same information from each candidate so that direct comparisons become possible and meaningful

Additional aims of interviewers could also include:

- demonstrating equality and fairness to each candidate in the process
- opening the negotiation of terms of employment between candidate and organisation

An interview meets these aims by:

✔ using an explicitly standardised process and evaluating applicants using the same criteria to make sure that the decision is as objective possible

✔ making sure that the content of the interview is clearly linked to job content

✔ giving a face-to-face opportunity to share more detailed information about the role, duties to be performed, and the employer's expectations

✔ giving candidates an opportunity to ask questions. Those that are able to do this are likely to leave with more information regarding the context and boundaries within which they would be expected to work

Interviews give the human interaction element to the recruitment process and very few recruiters feel confident in making decisions without conducting them. It's important to meet someone in person to fully assess his or her suitability for the job.

Lessons about interviews . . .

The traditional unstructured interview approach is now understood to be a poor predictor of actual job performance. Because such interviews were unstructured they were, naturally, different each time. This meant that some applicants got better opportunities to demonstrate their abilities than others. Even where similar questions were used, the criteria for evaluation changed from one applicant to the next because the judgments were subjective and not standardised between interviewers.

After 1970, equal opportunities legislation was introduced and the shortcomings of selection interviews were brought to light, sometimes very openly in court. Two areas where interviews improved as a result of these findings are:

- **procedural justice.** All candidates get the 'same chances' to get the job. In real terms, this means using exactly the same procedure in the same order for each candidate. Also, evaluations are made in the same way, using the same criteria. For example, each interviewee should be asked the same questions in the same order, and should be given the same amount of time to answer each question. Finally, the criteria must be factors that are related to successful job performance and the process requires no irrelevant factors.

■ **distributive justice.** All candidates are given equal chances to apply and to succeed and the best candidate gets the job.

. . . and the cost of getting it wrong

All managers should take selection interviewing seriously. If they hire people just on a gut feeling, their preferences and prejudices can lead to all sorts of problems, including:

■ immediate damage to the hiring manager's reputation if work is done poorly

■ delays in the delivery of products or services

■ drops in quality, which can result in customers deserting your business

■ risks to health and safety where employees are careless or incompetent

■ potential legal action against the organisation if candidates are not given a fair chance because of their race, gender, disability, religion, sexual orientation, or age

■ potential negative repercussions for the public. For example, if the job is a responsible one—a safety manager or a teacher, say—there could be wide-reaching knock-on effects if the wrong person gets the job.

TOP TIP

Remember that recruitment decisions affect the future as well as the present. If the wrong hiring decisions are made consistently over a period of time, the calibre of staff in your business will fall. The end result is a big impact on the bottom line.

Step two: Make sure you have structured interview training

Anyone who might be called on to conduct interviews should be given appropriate training. Awareness training, at a basic level, equips people to understand why a carefully designed and systematically implemented selection process is important. Those who may be involved in designing interviews should have in-depth training.

To improve fairness and the quality of selection decisions, and to avoid turning off good candidates, basic training of interviewers should cover:

- the importance of consistency among interviewers
- the reasons why consistency for all applicants is important
- why prepared questions should be clearly related to job performance (see Chapter 2)

- ■ how questions are carefully designed to maximise the effectiveness of interviews alongside other selection procedures such as screening and ability tests (see Chapter 2)
- ■ how to put the interviewee at ease so that information flows during the discussion, especially important where verbal communication is not important to the job (see Chapter 3)
- ■ why non-verbal behaviour—that is, body language— should be observed, but not given undue weight (see Chapter 3)
- ■ why interviewers should avoid talking too much (see Chapter 3)
- ■ that notes taken during an interview should be full and detailed (see Chapter 2)
- ■ why evaluations need to be tested to ensure that they are based on sound information rather than prejudice or assumption (see Chapter 7).

Common mistakes

✗ **You get distracted by grooming, attractiveness, and 'similar-to-me' effects**

Research has shown that on occasions where the applicant's dress—or even hairstyle—is similar to the interviewer's this can have a positive effect on their ratings, even when these factors will have no effect at all on their job performance. For women, the make-up or jewellery they wore was found to have the same effect.

The interviewer's perception that they are similar to the applicant was also related to their evaluations. To avoid this, using structured interviews forces interviewers to be very specific in their ratings and to back up their ratings with notes and examples. See Chapter 2 for more information.

✗ **Your view is skewed by the 'halo' effect, the 'contrast' effect, or 'first impression' error**

Even though we all strive to be as dispassionate as possible when it comes to rating interview candidates, it is possible to be subconsciously affected by events that take place during the interview. For example:

■ the **'halo' effect** occurs where a candidate answers very strongly—either positively or negatively—to one question. This makes such an impression on the interviewer that it's impossible to shift it from his or her mind when moving on to rate other answers

■ the **'contrast' effect** occurs when an impression continues to the next applicant: the interviewer allows the impression that the last applicant made influence the scores of the next applicant. For example, a mediocre applicant following a bad candidate may appear very good, but the same candidate may look very bad when compared to a good one

■ **'first impression' error** occurs where the interviewer makes a subjective evaluation early in the interview based on characteristics that are only marginally associated with job performance. He or she then rates all the answers given by the applicant on the basis of this first impression

The good news is that training, as well as scoring applicants' answers systematically, can cut down on the chances of your final decision being adversely affected by these factors.

STEPS TO SUCCESS

✔ Interviews are the most popular way of recruiting people. They *are* expensive, though, as they are time-consuming, so it really is worth putting in the effort to make sure you get the best result possible.

✔ Interviews still represent good value when they are run properly—especially if you take into account the potential cost of getting selection decisions wrong.

✔ When structured interviews are used systematically by trained personnel, the reliability and validity of the selection decision are improved.

✔ If you're responsible for overseeing interviews in your organisation, give training to all those who will be involved in the process. This will make sure that risky short cuts are not taken.

✔ If you have never interviewed someone before but you're asked to take part in one, ask for the training you need.

Useful links

Business Link (for small businesses; click through to the 'Employing people' section):
www.businesslink.gov.uk

Chartered Institute of Personnel and Development:
www.cipd.org.uk

Chartered Institute of Management:
www.managers.org.uk

Preparing to interview others

Once you're a manager, it's very likely that you'll be involved in the recruitment process at some point. You could be looking for a new assistant, for example, or asked to sit in with other colleagues as a 'second opinion' as they interview others.

If you're new to interviewing people, the following chapters will help you do the right groundwork before the interview so that you get as much out of it as you can. They'll help you work out the best questions to ask . . . and those to avoid like the plague.

If you've had some interviewing experience already but don't feel comfortable, read on to set your mind at rest and improve your skills. First of all, though, think back over past interviews you've conducted. What has your attitude to them been up to this point? Have you always prepared fully? Or have you retrieved the applicant's CV from under your coffee mug and interviewed using the questions that came into your head at that moment? If you did the latter, put those days behind you. In this section we look at how the modern structured approach to interviewing will help you get more objective, effective, and legally safer results.

Step one: Choose a criterion and baseline

The selection decisions

When you interview candidates, you're hoping to find out which applicants can do the job. When you have finished interviewing, you'll make a decision about whether to hire or whether you need to keep looking. If you have more successful applicants than job vacancies, you also need to decide who you think will do the job the best.

Ask yourself:

■ How will you know in the future whether you made good or bad selection decisions?
■ How will you know if your new interview process is making things better or worse?

A criterion is a measure of job performance that you use to tell you whether your selection decisions are good or bad. You need to choose a criterion and make a 'baseline' measurement now, before you change your interview process, so that you have something against which to check your success (or failure!).

For example:

Janet is aware of legislation changes and wants to update her selection process during interview procedures to ensure that in future she will:

- pick the very best staff for vacancies
- make sure that her process will not discriminate on the basis of age

She'll soon be expanding her team of customer advisors and believes that it should be possible to find good staff. Her existing team are knowledgeable enough but they are not motivated to help customers. In fact, they annoy customers with their attitude.

Janet decides to use the customer satisfaction rating measured by short questionnaires collected as customers leave. This will be the criterion. This is carried out at 3pm on the last Saturday of the month. She makes sure that she has figures as baseline measurements, then starts to design the new selection processes. Once the new team members have settled in, she can compare new ratings with the baseline ratings.

Step two: Work out your budget

Often people don't bother to think about how much they are willing to spend on the selection process. 'As little as possible', may be the answer in many cases. If you pause to think about the decisions you will be making and about the cost of getting it wrong (see Chapter 1), it focuses the mind a little more. Here are some questions to think about when making a selection decision:

- What is the nature of the vacancy?
- Is the vacancy a one-off, or will you be recruiting people for this position frequently?
- How many people do you need to recruit on this occasion?
- Is the job one of a family of similar roles?
- Does the role involve taking on responsibility?
- Does it involve any risk?
- Is it easy to find people willing to do this type of work?
- Do you need to improve on the selection decisions made on previous occasions?
- Will the role involve working with customers, or is it a back-office position?

Step three: Know what you are looking for

An interview is your chance to gather information so that you can compare candidates against job requirements and against each other. The first thing to do is to make sure that you know in detail what the job requirements are and how important each of them is to job performance.

A job analysis is a process for collecting information about what a job entails. It gives you a list of duties, tasks, and worker actions required. In brief, one way to do this is to ask job experts (for example: successful job incumbents, managers, and direct reports) to describe the actions that result in particularly effective performance of the job. Each job expert can usually give several direct examples of these. If you use this 'critical incident' job analysis technique, it also tells you which actions and attributes lead to high performance. You can also use this technique to find out which actions and attributes may lead to ineffective performance.

Make a note of how each skill or characteristic contributes to success in the role, especially if your interview process will be used repeatedly. You need to write down **how you know** that these strengths are important to job performance, since this will be needed when the interview process is reviewed in the future, or if a discrimination case is ever brought against your company.

This information ensures that the interviews you carry out will concentrate on important job-related attributes. This is key to a legally defensible selection process.

TOP TIP
**If appropriate, check in with colleagues to see
how they have done things. For example, if
you work in a large organisation, check
whether other branches or departments have
already carried out job analysis work for the**

---

same or similar roles. It may have been done for appraisal purposes, for a salary review or benchmarking activity. Don't waste your time duplicating work already done elsewhere.

Step four: Create a person specification

The job analysis gives you a list of duties, tasks, and actions. You can translate these into the knowledge, skills, and attributes that are used by the worker to carry out the job. You'll need to know the required level of each. Your job analysis information will help you to be specific about the threshold level and the level desirable. When you have finished this person specification, check back with your job experts.

Some requirements may be critical. You won't consider candidates without a threshold level. A common example of this might be basic number skills for a cashier's job. For some job requirements, the more the candidates show the better, for example, interest in the product for a sales person. Finally, you may need a particular amount of some attributes and more than the right amount may be a bad thing. An example of this could be confidence, where too much may be viewed as arrogance and ultimately be counterproductive.

Step five: Decide which tools to use

In this section, you'll need to look for tools that will predict the most important attributes for the job. The question is: 'which selection test or tool will help me to identify which candidates have exactly the attributes I'm looking for?'

Popular selection tools include:

■ CV with reference check
■ application forms with reference check
■ ability tests
■ personality inventories which identify personal preferences and characteristics
■ interviews
■ work sample tests, such as a presentation or a typing test

To increase the validity of the interview, you need to limit its scope. Don't try to cover everything with an interview. Not all criteria are best assessed by interview anyway.

The CV and/or application form can be used to work out whether candidates have a baseline level of some criteria. This then represents a first hurdle that applicants must pass to be considered further. When they're used in conjunction with reference checks to ensure accuracy, application forms are considered a reliable way to do this type of screening.

For the application form to be valid, it must measure factors that are *directly* related to job performance, such as previous relevant experience. Factors that predict desired worker behaviour may also increase validity. For example, if you have discovered that 'length of time in previous role' is predictive of cashiers' length of service, you can justify using this criteria from application forms or CVs, as it will help you reduce turnover in the long term. Reducing the number of applicants to a list of promising candidates will help to reduce the costs of the next stage.

In small organisations, expertise can usually be established through the interview process. In large organisations where there are frequent vacancies for a particular job type and normally HR personnel on hand to administer them, expertise is better measured using a specific knowledge or skill test. Work-related tests can be used to assess job knowledge too.

When several tests are to be used, candidates are often invited to an assessment centre, where they will all be intensively tested, assessed, and interviewed over the course of a day or two. This is most common in large organisations. Where this is the case, the issue of meals and tours of the office comes up. Inform candidates if they are to be observed during a meal or a tour and then structure them so that all candidates have as far as possible the same experience. If you decide to make them informal, then let candidates know that the meal or tour is not part of the selection process and ensure that someone who is not involved in the selection decision performs the role of host.

Interviews are the most effective tools for measuring interpersonal skills and the characteristics related to trustworthiness, resilience, and integrity. Limit the scope of your interview to two or three of the most relevant criteria that fall into these categories.

Step six: Plan your questions

When you know what your basic criteria are, prepare several questions for each of them. Take care to write open questions that encourage candidates to give you information and talk about their experiences: you won't discover very much if all a candidate can say is 'yes' or 'no'!

Situation-based questions ask candidates to tell you how they would respond in a hypothetical situation that you describe. An example might be: 'You're just about to sign off from your shift when a customer makes a complaint about the safety of a display in the store. What would you do?'

Behaviour-based questions ask candidates to talk about past situations similar to those they will come across if they get the job. This allows you to assess either their typical performance or best performance, depending on the wording of the question, which comes in two parts. First you ask the candidate to recall a situation similar to the one you describe, then you ask some probing questions that allow you to assess what actions they took and the results of their actions. An example might be:

■ Tell me about a situation where you were particularly persuasive.

The probing questions might be:

■ What actions did you take?
■ How many others were involved?
■ What part did you play yourself?
■ How successful were you?
■ What did you learn as a result?

Step seven: Design answer-rating records

Many people find it helpful to have a 'scorecard' when they're interviewing—see below for an example. It can help them write notes and award each candidate 'points' depending on how well they match up to person specification, and improves consistency and fairness.

Each question should be rated separately as it is answered. Leave room to write after each question, as this prompts the interviewer to take useful notes about each candidate's answer and these notes may help decide between two applicants at the end of the process. The example below demonstrates what this can look like, with the rating and interviewer's observations:

Q1. Can you tell me about the most recent time when you worked with a team?

- How many people were working on it?
- What role did you play?
- What was the task?
- How did you have an effect on the results?
- Were there any barriers or obstacles?
- How did you overcome them?
- How successful were the results?

1	2	3	4	5
Not effective or unused to working in a team	Worked as a team member before, no notable success	Understood their team role and worked effectively	Led a team or very effective team member in successful team	Highly effective leader and very flexible and highly effective team member

Rating and notes: 4

Paul worked as a team member, monitoring casual workers' safety on three sites. Was effective at his own role and ensured the safety of other workers too by challenging the foremen where necessary, including standing up to a 'nasty piece of work'. Barrier: was not always there as multiple sites but delegated effectively to reps and led them well. Good communicator within the team about possible problems etc. No serious accidents or injuries reported. Not 5 because Paul is not used to leading a team.

Step eight: Review the process

Look back over the process that you have designed. If you're interviewing with other people, you might want to draw up a simple chart of some kind that can help you explain the process to others. You could also use it as a checklist to make sure that you've thought through all the logistics, including allowing plenty of time to contact interview candidates.

It's extremely important that the process you use is both fair and lawful. There are many legal requirements in place to protect our employment rights and these regulations currently include:

- The Equal Pay Act 1970
- The Sex Discrimination Act 1975
- The Race Relations Act 1976, amended in 2000
- The Disability Discrimination Act 1995, amended in 2004
- The Employment Rights Act
- Employment Equality (Sexual Orientation) Regulations 2003
- Employment Equality (Religion or Belief) Regulations 2003

- The Human Rights Act 1998
- Age legislation is due to be implemented late in 2006

Legislation is subject to changes and amendments, so for up-to-date detailed information on avoiding discrimination, visit the Equal Opportunities Commission or the Department for Trade and Industry websites (addresses below).

Do not add unnecessary requirements: they could exclude people unfairly, which is unlawful. If in doubt, talk to recent recruits to gather feedback about how they found the recruitment process. Although they may not have the full picture, they may have helpful comments or ideas on how the integrity and fairness of the system can be improved.

Make sure that any job advertisement, descriptions, or person specifications are worded appropriately. Also invite candidates to tell you about special needs relating to any disability before participating in interviews and tests. Make sure that you ask candidates, as part of the interview process, what adjustments to work premises, practices, or equipment can be made to enable him/her to do the job. This will save any embarrassment or difficulty for them or you and ensures that you are complying with the law.

The Access to Work programme run by the Department of Work and Pensions may be able to help with special equipment, alterations to premises, travel assistance and so on. To find out more, contact your nearest Jobcentre.

Common mistakes

✗ You give a poor first impression of your company

The best rooms in which to hold interviews are quiet, light, and airy, with a comfortable temperature and no distractions. If you use the broom cupboard on the landing of your oldest building where you know that parking will be a problem, you're hardly going to attract the best candidates to take a job with you. Remember that you are presenting your opening bid in the negotiation. Prepare to talk to candidates about why you joined the organisation and what keeps you loyal. Explain the company vision and how you see your part in that. If at all possible, give candidates an attractive information pack that they can take away and read at their leisure, making sure that it addresses all the key issues they will want to know about.

✗ You're inconsistent in the way you treat the candidates

It's important that you're fair to the interview candidates by treating them consistently. Interview each person in the same room and under the same conditions. Make sure you won't be disturbed: put a sign on the door if you have to. Before you start, turn off your mobile phone and ask candidates to do the same with theirs. Keep a close eye on the time and keep to your schedule as far as you possibly can.

✗ The room layout is intimidating

Try to use the furniture to your advantage: don't glare at your candidates from behind a desk—it's unnecessarily intimidating. Move your chair to one side, so you can both use one corner of the desk for coffee or notes, without feeling that it is a barrier. Don't forget to smile, be positive, and be enthusiastic about your business.

STEPS TO SUCCESS

✔ Start by choosing a criterion measure so that you can compare the results of your new selection process against the results of what you did before.

✔ Think about your budget in the light of what poor decisions could cost you.

✔ Don't just guess what you are looking for. Use job analysis information to guide you to which factors really contribute to great job performance.

✔ It is best not to rely on interview alone. Interviews are best at measuring personal characteristics like integrity, rapport, and communication.

✔ The way that questions are designed has been shown to be very important to validity. Ensure that your questions really get at the factors you want to measure.

✔ Answer records and rating scales with 'descriptive anchors' are a good way to ensure interviewer consistency.

Useful links

Business Link:
www.businesslink.gov.uk
Equal Opportunities Commission:
www.eoc.org.uk
Department of Trade and Industry:
www.dti.gov.uk

Conducting a one-to-one interview

Now that you've prepared carefully, you can be confident that your interview process is as good as it can be. In this section you'll learn how to run the interview, staying in control of the process, while keeping the atmosphere relaxed and businesslike.

Step one: Put the candidate at ease

Starting with a smile every time, stating that you are pleased that the candidate was able to attend, can make a big difference. Smiling and making eye contact relaxes you and connects you with the person you are talking to. This helps the conversation to flow, which is vital if you are to gather information from the candidate. Remember, you are trying to keep the process consistent, so make smiling a habit when you greet interviewees.

Explain the process that each candidate will be experiencing and emphasise that each person will be going through the exact same set-up. If people know the format, they're much more likely to relax, focus their mind on the questions, and speak more freely. It's good practice to check before you start that any special needs have been noted and that any required adjustments have been made.

Personal (but not *too* personal) space

'Personal space' is the expression used to describe the zone around your body that you are subconsciously aware of. It can be uncomfortable to try to hold a conversation with someone who is either invading your personal space, or who someone who is outside the usual territorial zone.

These zones depend very much on context, culture, and relationships. When you are greeting people and when you are laying out your interview room, think carefully about how you are using space and the effect this may have on others. In the UK the zones (and who you allow into them) are roughly as follows:

- intimate zone (15–46 cm): relatives, close friends
- personal zone (46–126 cm): colleagues that you like and trust, friends
- social zone (1.2–3.6 m): new colleagues, strangers, people you don't trust

Step two: Use your prepared question format

The next stage of the interview should see you settle into a relaxed but businesslike attitude. You need to encourage the candidate to give you information while making it clear that there is a structure that you are in control of. It's important that you stick to the process that you planned, since that creates a level playing field for all candidates.

Having said that, interviewers are permitted to go beyond the set questions to check or clarify understanding, to probe deeper for important details, or to pursue closely related areas. The prepared questions act as a script and ensure the consistency and validity of the process.

New interviewers may find it tricky to keep one part of their mind on the process of the interview while listening carefully to the candidate to rate the content of what they are saying. Practise interviewing a friend or colleague, so you are ready for the real applicants. Alternatively, arrange for an observer to help with ratings and notes until you are confident of your interviewing skills. But remember that conditions should be the same for each person you interview.

TOP TIP
Remember that you want to find out more about the candidate, not listen to yourself for an hour. The best way of doing this is to ask 'open' questions—ones that can't be answered with just 'yes' or 'no'. Read on to find out more about encouraging candidates to speak freely.

Step three: Manage chatty candidates

You may need to stop candidates from straying off topic, as some people find it hard to stick to the point when they are nervous. Red herrings can make a mess of your timing for other questions. As soon as you notice that the candidate is straying, redirect their focus. For example, you can say 'Can I stop you there, we may cover that later. Can you tell me about . . .?'

When your interviewee has a lot to say, you can slightly alter your questions to focus them better on the area you want to cover. For example:

- 'Can you tell me *concisely* about . . .?'
- '*Precisely*, what was your role?'
- 'What were the results of your actions, *in brief*?'

It's a lot harder to find the right words when you're nervous. Try to strike a balance between moving the interview on and putting the applicant at ease. If the interviewee still responds with long, rambling answers, tell them that you have a lot to cover and politely ask them to be more concise.

TOP TIP

Sometimes you will find that a candidate simply loses the thread of what they are saying. If you are taking notes—and you should be!—you can remind them of the

---

**question they were answering and tell them
briefly what points they have made, allowing
them to pick up where they left off.**

Step four: Manage quiet candidates

Some candidates will be quieter than usual because they
are nervous. Be tactful and reassuring. Don't be afraid of
pauses, as some people take a moment to think before
they answer. Some good ways of getting them to open
up include:

- using encouraging noises such as 'aha' or 'mmm'
- using short phrases like: 'I see and then . . .?' or 'Tell me
  more . . .'
- asking additional questions if you need more
  information

TOP TIP

**If you use the route above, don't be tempted
to lead the interviewee or ask 50:50 questions
(where the candidate can choose between
two answers that you have given them): the
whole point is to get them to tell you their
reaction to something, not mimic yours.**

Occasionally you will get a candidate who goes completely
blank. Make sure you are prepared for this. A nervous

candidate may become very distressed, which makes answering still more difficult. The job is probably very important to them if they are very nervous about it.

Nerves versus capability

It's important to remember that the best candidate is not always relaxed or confident at interview.

Your job as interviewer is to get nervous candidates back on track so that they can demonstrate their knowledge, skills, and abilities to you. Here's how to do it:

- ✓ stay calm yourself
- ✓ be reassuring; tell them to take their time and then restate the question in a relaxed tone of voice
- ✓ check that they understand the question. You may have used a word that they don't understand or their response may be 'it depends'
- ✓ if they become distressed, reassure them that it's OK, suggest they take some deep breaths while you get them a glass of water
- ✓ try moving on to another question, saying you'll come back to the other question at the end. Then calmly restart the interview with the next question you planned to ask
- ✓ alternatively, you can use information from their CV or application form as a 'starter' to get a modest or shy candidate talking. For example: 'This question is about leading projects. Did you lead any at XYZ Consulting? Tell me a bit about one of them.' You can

then go back to your original question, if you felt it was
unanswered, as the candidate will be more into his or
her stride.

Step five: Learn to listen

Before the interview, clear your mind. Try not to think
about the previous candidate while you are interviewing
the next one. It is especially important in the first few minutes
to focus your attention on the person in front of you. Let
them know that you are doing that by maintaining eye
contact with them while you introduce the structure of the
interview and while you ask the first question. You will then
need to start taking notes but keep looking up to make eye
contact that will reassure your interviewee that you are
listening and interested. Don't let your notes become a
barrier to good communication; you do need to take them,
but you should leave yourself ten minutes between
candidates to flesh out your notes. This may take practice,
so leave more time between interviews while you are new
to it.

TOP TIP

**Don't let external distractions get in the
way of meaningful communication. Make
sure that you are both facing away from
windows if traffic may distract you.
Remember, other work has to wait.**

While listening to and rating the content of each answer, read with your eyes and ears the messages 'between the lines'. What is the message? Don't jump to conclusions about what someone's body language is saying—people are hardly going to be acting naturally in an interview situation—but you will easily be able to tell whether a person talks about a subject with relish and enthusiasm, or whether they are reluctant to go into depth about something.

Avoid talking too much yourself. Sticking to your prepared format will help with this. Try not to finish people's sentences or you may end up rating yourself rather than what the interviewee has said! Check that you have understood correctly by reflecting back to the candidate—in your own words—what you have learned in summary (for example, 'So, you've worked in sales for three years and have been managing a team of two other people for the past year'). If you are not sure what the interviewee is saying, ask further questions until you are clear. When you ask additional questions, make sure that you are not leading them to a particular answer.

Step six: Give feedback if requested

Candidates will often ask for feedback as it will help them improve their self-presentation. Many companies consider it good practice to give feedback where possible. If you have time, at the end of each interview change pens and jot down in a different colour a few quick notes that you can use to give feedback. If you do this while the interview is fresh in your mind, it won't take long to add a feedback paragraph to rejection letters. This will help candidates to understand why they didn't get the job and what they need to do to improve.

When did *you* last get feedback on how you come across? Think about your interviewing skills, listening techniques, and body language. Also:

■ Could candidates find you cold and intimidating, polite and professional, or are you embarrassingly over-cheerful and gushy?
■ How clear did they find your questions?
■ Have you fallen into bad habits, such as cutting across what a nervous interviewee is saying or allowing ramblers to stray from the subject?

Common mistakes

✗ You don't make enough notes

It's likely that at the end of the interviewing process, you'll need to discuss the merits of each candidate with colleagues. As part of that, you'll need examples from candidates' answers. The selection decision will come from your ratings, backed up by your notes. If you cannot say why you made a particular rating, it could be embarrassing. Worse, if a discrimination case is brought against you, you will need your notes for your defence.

✗ You ignore the legislation aimed at combating discrimination

Employment legislation changes all the time and if you've not informed yourself about the current state of play, you might come unstuck at some stage. All it takes is a poorly phrased question to land you in trouble. What you must do is avoid inappropriate questions at interview. In the United Kingdom, these include (but are not restricted to):

- Are you married, divorced, or single?
- Are you planning to start a family?
- Do you have children? How old are they?
- Will your partner move if we offer you this job?
- How would you feel working for a white female boss?
- Why would a woman want a job like this?
- What provisions have you made for childcare?
- How will you cope with travel bearing in mind you're confined to a wheelchair?
- How will you cope with customers on the phone in English as it's your second language?
- What is your religious faith?
- Does your religion prevent you from working at weekends?
- How old are you? What is your date of birth?

Visit the Department of Trade and Industry website (address below) for more information on what questions to avoid during an interview.

✗ You're tempted to try to 'get round' the legislation

The legislation is there because in the past people who might have done a job well were **unfairly** ruled out, either through prejudice or indirect discrimination.

Having said that, there are some questions related to personal circumstances, such as physical ability, previous convictions or religion, which might not be discriminatory but you need to make sure that you ask in a suitable and professional way.

For example, you may need to find out what adjustments need to be made to give easy access to an applicant with a disability. You may phrase a question: 'How will we need to adjust your working area to ensure that you can do the work?' or 'What specialist equipment will help you to carry out the job?' Some interviewers will prefer to deal with these questions completely separately from the interview.

✗ You focus on selling the job and the company

Research has found that selling the job during interview is a very expensive and ineffective use of time. Interviewees are attracted more by the way that they are treated at interview than by what you say about the organisation and the role. Put together an attractive pack of information that they can read and refer to after their interview instead of devoting interview time to presenting. (You'll still need to be ready to answer any questions that the interviewees might have for you there and then, however.) Make sure that all the candidates are greeted warmly so that their first impressions are favourable and take the time to thank them properly for attending before you say goodbye.

STEPS TO SUCCESS

✔ Start by building rapport with your interviewee so that the conversation flows more easily. Show some empathy and remember how difficult it is to perform at your best when you are nervous.

✔ Think about personal space and take care not to invade others' personal zone.

✔ Stick to your prepared questions so that you can make sure that everyone is treated in the same way. You can, of course, ask extra questions to clarify something if appropriate or probe areas deeper to gain a better picture, depending on what each candidate says to you.

✔ Don't allow candidates to waffle on or take you too far 'off piste'. If you feel someone is wandering, politely but firmly refocus them on the question.

✔ A quiet candidate is the most difficult to interview—an interview is supposed to be a conversation, after all! Use your interpersonal skills to encourage candidates to talk and remember to ask 'open' questions.

✓ Candidates' minds may go blank when nervous. If this happens, give them the time they need to re-gather their thoughts. If they cannot answer, skip on to the next question and come back to the problem one at the end.

✓ Great listeners develop through feedback and practice. Make sure you get plenty of both.

✓ Make sure your process is lawful. Check that you and any other interviewers know what you can and cannot ask at interview.

Useful links

Department of Trade and Industry:
www.dti.gov.uk
Equal Opportunities Commission:
www.eoc.org.uk

Taking part in a panel interview

In a panel interview, you invite candidates to present themselves to a group. This may be just two or three people, or include as many as ten. The goal of the panel interview is the same as it is for a one-to-one interview: to gather enough relevant information from the candidates to make a good selection decision. Panel interviews are most common in large organisations, but it is still useful to know how they can fit in to the bigger picture even if you run your own business. You could be asked to participate in a panel interview elsewhere, for example, or if your business is expanding and you want to recruit a new key member of staff, you may want to ask others help you make the final decision.

Whatever your situation, read on to find more about best practice in panel interviews.

Step one: Understand the purpose of a panel interview

This style of interview is used to get relevant information about candidates *from different viewpoints*. Some jobs require you to work across different functions—marketing, sales, and PR, for example—so many people have a stake in the right person being chosen. The panel interview is used to reveal different aspects of candidates' knowledge, skills, expertise, or other attributes.

Organisations commonly use panel interviews to whittle down a shortlist of candidates for top-level executive posts. The benefit is that representatives of each department can ask questions to find out whether the candidates could cope with the multifunctional duties of the role. Finally, they can be used in situations where it is critical that the jobholder can communicate well with different groups under pressure. This last instance is the only situation where a panel can allow themselves to be other than warm and welcoming.

TOP TIP

Think carefully about who should take part in a panel interview. You need to make sure you have a representative from each relevant part of the organisation as well as a good mix of people with interviewing experience. Make sure that all those who need it get plenty of training in advance.

Step two: Avoid discrimination

If you've skipped straight to this chapter, it's extremely important that you avoid asking questions that are discriminatory. Asking unlawful or politically incorrect questions will—at best—make you look unprofessional. At worst, it could land you in court. Make sure you know about the relevant legislation around issues of equality (see Chapters 2 and 3), and check that the questions you ask are lawful and can be justified.

Keep in mind that you are looking for the very best candidate. Wipe away any preconceptions of what that candidate will look like or which segment of society he or she will come from. When you are focused properly on relevant factors to the job, such as knowledge, ability, skills, personality, and potential, you'll apply the selection criteria fairly.

Step three: Know your own role and prepare for it

To be effective, all panel members need to understand where they fit in to the scheme. They also need to understand how important the process is to ensuring the validity and reliability of the selection decision. It can be tempting for managers to introduce 'pet criteria' that have not been researched, such as 'thinks outside the box' or 'will fit in' late in the day, or even during the interview, if not briefed properly.

Find out your role in advance, including the specific criteria that you are there to check out, then plan your questions to get the information you need from the candidates. If you are not sure how to go about this, Chapters 1 and 2 will help. If you are still in doubt and your organisation is large enough, ask for training or one-to-one help from the personnel department. If you work for (or run) a small organisation, you'll be able to get specific help from Business Link advisers.

Step three: Take responsibility

If you are responsible for planning the panel interview, here are some points to help you.

✔ Let candidates know in advance that part of the process will be a panel interview and, where possible, *who* will be on the interview committee. This allows them to prepare themselves properly for the experience.

✔ Make sure panel members are well briefed and have the information they require in plenty of time so they can prepare. They will need to know the job title and description as well as the person specification. Also give them a copy of the job advertisement and all CVs.

✔ Make it very clear which criteria you are asking them to cover, what level of the criteria is required, and whether others will also be covering these.

✔ They need to know the schedule as early as possible, so they can make time in their diary. Schedule time in panel members' diaries the day after panel interviews to debrief and make a decision.

✔ Ask panel members to give you their questions in advance. This may not be popular, but allows you to plan the order in which questions will be asked and check that the interview will meet best practice requirements.

✔ Prepare a rating 'scorecard' (see Chapter 2). You'll need enough copies for each interviewer to have a fresh one for each interviewee. Make sure that they are clearly marked in advance with the interviewer's and interviewee's names.

✔ Reiterate the importance of notes and ratings when you brief the panel before the first interview and remind panel members that the interviewee can ask to see their notes under the Data Protection Act.

✔ When you meet each candidate, don't forget to smile warmly and thank him or her for attending. You can do this with some sincerity, since several people would be twiddling their thumbs if they hadn't turned up!

✔ Panel interviews tend to be more formal than one-to-one interviews, so make sure that you give candidates a chance to settle in by introducing everyone and giving an overview of how you'll proceed before allowing the first question.

✔ Remember, if you are chairing the interview, you can wrap up by asking if anyone needs clarification of any points before asking the interviewee if he or she has any questions to ask the panel.

✔ If you can give some guidance to candidates about the timescale for decisions it is wise to do so. Of course you must then stick to what you have said or contact interviewees and apologise for any delay. Candidates who have been kept waiting for a rejection decision rarely speak highly of an organisation.

✔ Finally, when the contract is signed, don't forget to pat yourself and your panel on the back. Panel interviews are time consuming and costly but they are worth it for a good selection decision.

Common Mistakes

✗ The interview turns into an interrogation

Panels have been known to forget the purpose of the interview and compete with each other to ask the most difficult questions or to pile on the pressure. A 'stress interview' is occasionally required where one of the job criteria is to cope with pressure. When this is the case, a specialist should design a process so that the same pressure can be put on each candidate. It is, however, very easy to get the process wrong and this can be disastrous for the organisation's reputation. Again, good briefing should make sure this does not happen to your panel.

✗ You rush the decision

After a long day of interviewing, don't expect your panel to make a good decision. If they want to get away to their family or leisure pursuits, panel members will make a quick, rather than a good, decision. If you are doing the scheduling, make time during the day for them to flesh out notes between interviews. Schedule a meeting the next morning to discuss candidates and make decisions, when the panel can give their full attention.

Where there is pressure to hire, the 'halo effect' described in Chapter 1 is particularly likely to play a part in poor decisions. A candidate makes a good first impression or is strong on the first answer. The panel go onto autopilot and make positive evaluations of subsequent answers, rather than listening and rating carefully. Again, a good briefing and a proper scorecard with descriptive anchors will help panel members to guard against this.

STEPS TO SUCCESS

✔ A panel interview uses a group to gather job-related information from a candidate from different perspectives.

✔ If you're taking part in a panel interview, it's important that you know your role so that you can prepare good quality questions as you would for other interviews.

✔ Make sure that you know which questions you cannot ask and why.

✔ Proper briefing will ensure that the panel are consistent in the way they treat all the candidates.

✔ If you're chairing a panel interview, take care that the interview doesn't descend into an interrogation. This isn't the time for panel members to show off by trying to ask the hardest question possible.

✔ Put in place a sensible process for comparing notes on candidates. This will make sure that all your evaluations are fair as well as thorough.

Useful links

Business Link:
www.businesslink.gov.uk
Everything HR related:
www.hr-guide.com
Institute of Business Ethics:
www.ibe.org.uk

Conducting a telephone interview

Telephone interviews are on the increase because they are a cost-effective way to carry out screening. The Chartered Institute of Personnel and Development (CIPD) estimated that in 2004 a quarter of organisations used phone interviews. The aims and rules of interviewing are the same for this type of interview as for any other, but in this chapter we explain how you can get information quickly and effectively by telephone.

Step one: Understand the telephone interview in context

Telephone interviews are becoming increasingly popular, particularly as an initial 'sifting' phase of applicants before any are invited to a face-to-face interview. They can take the form of:

- **the 'informal chat'.** This can take in a brief discussion of various aspects of the role and the employer organisation. It can also be a low-key way of gauging the candidate's ability and willingness to do the work involved when, where, and how the business wants.

- **short, structured interviews.** Once a CV or application form has been received, a telephone interview can be used to screen candidates and create a shortlist. This will be based on key criteria that are 'deal breakers'. A deal breaker is a characteristic that candidates *must* have in order to be considered for the post. For example, for jobs that involve leading a team, it's likely that prior leadership experience would be helpful. If it's not clear from a candidate's CV whether she or he has led a team in previous employment (or whether they'd just been part of one), a short telephone interview will clear this up quickly.
- **longer, in-depth interviews.** These are often used for high-level positions in multinational companies. They are a way of whittling down the applicants to a shortlist of candidates who are invited to fly in for the final stage of selection.

Telephone interviews are often used when client confidentiality is an important issue. For example, a recruitment agency might use them to draw up a shortlist of candidates before revealing the client organisation to potential applicants.

TOP TIP

Where telephone skills are important for the job, as they are in telesales, a business may rely heavily on telephone interviews. Some businesses have even automated the process for large-scale recruitment. Recorded

---

questions are asked and multiple-choice answers given: the candidate keys in their responses via the keypad on their phone.

Step two: Think about the advantages . . .

The telephone interview does have several advantages over face-to-face interviews.

✔ It can speed up the time needed to get to a shortlist of candidates.

✔ Where a big response to an advertisement is expected, it's sometimes the only practical way to screen the large numbers of candidates.

✔ The outcome is known sooner, so the applicant is 'in limbo' for a shorter time.

✔ There is generally less disruption, as candidates do not need to travel and the interviewer does not need to book the rooms and the support that face-to-face interviews require.

✔ It gives rich information about the telephone skills of interviewees.

✔ It helps impartiality as the interviewer is basing his or her ratings of candidates purely on how they come across on the phone, rather than on how they look.

✔ Interviewers can record the interview **as long as they seek permission from the candidate**: this leaves them free to concentrate on assessing the candidate against the job criteria, rather than on taking notes.

Step three: . . . but don't forget the drawbacks

There are still some limitations to using the phone for interviews.

- It can be tempting to pick up the phone and have an unstructured, 'informal chat', which isn't a reliable way to choose the right person for the job.
- Interviewers may have preferences for certain accents or prejudices against others. While these discriminations may happen unwittingly, they're nonetheless unfair.
- Pauses seem longer on the telephone. Because you can't see someone's body language if they're not in the room with you, interviewers may misinterpret a pause and the dialogue may feel uncomfortable.
- Candidates find it harder to gauge how successful they are, as they do not have the visual 'clues' to read that they would have in a face-to-face interview. While this may not seem important to the interviewer, it may mean that you get a different evaluation than you would get in a one-to-one.
- Applicants have to wait for a chance to visit the worksite and meet the team they will be working with until later in

the process. If they don't like what they see, they may drop out at a later stage.

- Some candidates may have more distractions in the background than others, making the interview more difficult for them. Distractions and interruptions are a source of inconsistency that is harder to manage with telephone interviews.
- How can you be certain of the identity of the applicant over the phone? As with remote testing, you need to be sure that you are assessing the applicant.

Step four: Plan a short, structured interview

Before you start, be very clear about what *this stage* of the interview process is for. What do you aim to achieve with the telephone interview?

Typically, you want to give some information to the candidate and check that they are still interested in the role. For example, you may need IT staff to be available for callout on alternate weekends. Some applicants may opt out once they know this, so you have saved time interviewing people who would not be interested in the role.

Next you want to check whether the candidate meets a few crucial criteria that you have identified as important to the job role but which are not covered by the CV or application process. Keep to the consistency rule outlined in previous chapters so that each candidate gets the same questions and information. Take great care not to ask discriminatory questions (see Chapter 2).

Prepare enough information about the role to answer candidates' most basic questions. You can let applicants know what the next step is if they are successful and how long it will take for them to hear of your decision.

When you're ready to interview, arrange a suitable time with candidates. Ask them to confirm the number you should call them on and advise them to take the call in a quiet environment with no distractions.

Remember that candidates may not want their current employer to know that they're looking for a new job, so do be discreet if you're calling them at work. If you are calling someone at their home number, you must call at the time arranged—he or she may have taken time off work to talk to you. Be careful to treat candidates well: if you muck them about or make life difficult, you'll be giving a poor impression of your company. You want to attract the best candidates and maintain your organisation's good reputation.

Step five: Use good telephone techniques

Your voice creates 80% of your impact when you're on the phone. If you're not doing the interviewing yourself, make sure that you pick interviewers who come across very clearly on the telephone and who are good at picking the right words to create a good impression. They'll also need to have excellent interviewing skills, particularly at creating rapport and at meaningful listening.

You might like to try the following when you are making calls:

✔ SMILE! Your voice will be more positive and energetic if you smile as you talk. A smile also helps you to relax, and this will come across in your voice too.

✔ Introduce yourself clearly by stating your name. If the person answering the phone does not state their name, ask who you are speaking to, before you say more about why you are calling or the organisation you are calling from in case you are talking to a colleague or a house-mate. Discretion is important at all stages of the interview process, so start out as you mean to go on.

✔ Be ready to answer questions as well as to ask them: an interview is a two-way process and proactive candidates may have a lot they want to find out about you and your organisation.

✔ Keep notes of what the candidate says, at the same time as assessing them. These points can be very helpful if they lose their thread, as you can recap where the conversation had been going. These notes will also form the basis of your defence should your organisation ever be accused of unfair discrimination at interview.

✔ Speak a little more slowly than you would normally to make sure that the applicant understands you.

✔ Sometimes you might find that there is a lot of background noise at the candidate's end—it may be hard for them to find somewhere quiet to speak to you at the time you want. If you can tell that the candidate is in a noisy environment or is distracted, suggest that they phone you back when they have dealt with the noise or distraction. It would be a pity to dismiss a good candidate because they cannot hear your questions or give their answers their full attention.

TOP TIP

If you are new to telephone interviews, get some feedback on your telephone techniques so that you brush up on your skills before you start ringing candidates. You could also record yourself speaking to someone and review the result. Many people find that they speak a lot quicker than they realise— especially if they're nervous—so this could be one thing to look out for.

Common Mistakes

✘ **You don't speak clearly enough**

Talking too fast or mumbling into the telephone will make it very hard for the interviewee to be sure of what you are

---

asking. If you are asked to repeat your question more than once, you probably need to do something to make your questions clearer. Common problems are holding the telephone with your fingers over the microphone, holding the microphone too far under your chin, or pressing your chin against the microphone. Hands-free phones can be very useful—you'll be able to make notes much more easily for example—but they do pick up background noises, so be careful about shuffling your notes. Think about the ergonomics. If you are spending long periods on the phone it may be a good idea to use a headphone or earpiece to save you having your neck at an awkward angle when you're taking notes. Both are available quite cheaply.

✗ You place too much store by the candidates' telephone techniques

If you are recruiting for a post where use of the phone is *not* central, don't dismiss someone out of hand if their phone skills aren't fantastic. You may be discriminating unfairly against people with a disability, as well as those who simply do not come across well on the phone. Communication is a key part of many jobs, but focus on the job in question and be open-minded about each candidate.

✗ You don't plan the interview

If you're assessing people for interview selection purposes, you must use a fair process. This means that you have to plan the interview and write questions that

ensure each candidate gets the same interview and
that you are assessing job-related factors *only*.

STEPS TO SUCCESS

✔ Telephone interviews are now very common and can be
extremely useful, especially where good phone skills are
critical to the job vacancy.

✔ They are cost-effective, cutting down on travel costs and
general disruption.

✔ If your organisation is expecting a large response to a job
advertisement, using telephone interviews can help
focus selection resources on the candidates judged to
be best suited to the role.

✔ Make sure that telephone interviewers come up with—
and stick to—a question 'script', to make sure that all
candidates are being treated consistently.

✔ As with any job interview, make sure that you are a good
advertisement for your organisation. Be polite,
professional, and discreet: remember that the
candidates probably won't want to advertise the fact
that they are job-hunting to their existing boss, so don't
drop them in it.

✔ Whether you're interviewing over the phone yourself or
asking someone else to do it for you, remember that

interviewers need to have excellent telephone skills
themselves in order to do a good job.

 Speak clearly, listen carefully, and take notes as you go.

Useful link

Recruitment, retention and turnover survey by CIPD:
www.cipd.co.uk/surveys

Conducting an internal interview

Very often, when a job opportunity comes up, people from within the organisation, as well as outside it, want to apply.

The employment market has changed from the traditional apprentice-journeyman-master model to a fluid 'talent market'. Switching organisations no longer has a stigma attached and company loyalty is rarely lifelong. In fact, smart employees are reinventing themselves as free agents. Competition to obtain the best employees in the market is fierce.

While it's widely understood that recruiting top talent leads to better returns for an organisation, holding onto that talent—and using it in the right way in the right places within an organisation—is less well understood.

The concept of a 'strong bench', borrowed from football, is also useful here. It means that the pool of talent in the business needs to be constantly added to, so that future leaders are ready for the challenges they will face. Internal promotions are crucial to ensuring that people continue to find their jobs challenging and

fulfilling and feel valued because they do
important and interesting work.

Step one: Treat an internal interview just like any other

An internal interview is for an applicant who is already
employed by the organisation. To ensure that all applicants
have equal conditions, internal applicants should go through
the same process as external applicants.

Because internal applicants have already been selected for
their potential, they are a great asset to the organisation.
They have been trained and coached on the job and have
picked up a huge amount of knowledge relevant to the
organisation. They are a valuable investment and resource
for tomorrow—if the business can hold onto them—and
as such they deserve to be treated with great diplomacy.
If they get personal attention in the communication that
takes place around the interview and receive careful
feedback that links into development plans, they're less
likely to feel undervalued, discouraged, or discredited if
they don't get the job. In other words, they're more likely
to stay on. It is far cheaper to retain your existing
workforce than be continually filling vacancies. Recent
estimates from the CIPD suggest that the average cost
of recruiting and retraining a new staff member is close to
£5,000.

Step two: Pick the right internal interviewers

If you're responsible for selecting internal interviewers, you need to look for unbiased people to have any chance of a reliable and valid selection decision. It's generally accepted that the more pre-interview information an interviewer has about candidates, the less accurate the results are. It seems wise, then, to exclude any interviewers who have previous knowledge of the internal applicants, to avoid either positive or negative bias.

In a small organisation, or where there are few trained interviewers available, it may not be possible to avoid interviewing someone you know already. In this situation, be aware of a possible conflict of interest, but stick to the same procedure as for external candidates. Arrange for an observer to attend and monitor proceedings. Alternatively, if you have worked closely with the internal candidate, you may already have the information you need about their recent experience. However, you may still find it useful to interview them about their experiences prior to this.

TOP TIP
Even though internal candidates are known to you already, try not to give them an unfair advantage: it could hurt your business in the long run. Sometimes you may find better talent outside the organisation,

---

even though although an internal candidate could probably do the job. You have to weigh up the benefits of attracting and recruiting the best talent with the possibility of upsetting a good employee.

If you are responsible for personnel-related matters in your organisation, remember that not training interviewers properly is a false economy. If your company is small or cash-strapped, it could seem like an unnecessary expense, but if poorly trained interviewers make mistakes in selecting the right person, the cost implications of failure on the job can be great. The cost of high-quality specialist training can look very small when weighed in the balance.

In theory, those in charge of selection and in charge of development need to work together. It's their responsibility to increase the calibre of employees and they can do this best if they have a good understanding of each others' roles. Proper assessment procedures allow the organisation to select the best available talent for the role. Money spent wisely on developing people to play to their strengths while giving them challenges at the right level will make sure that their potential is realised.

For the purpose of retaining talent, put your best interviewers on the job for internal interviews. The process will then be up to scratch and also *intrinsically* motivating for the candidates. This means that employees find the process and the learning from it challenging and interesting (which they will if it is relevant and well designed), making it more likely that the internal candidates will respect the result and put themselves forward again in the future if they're not successful on this occasion.

Step three: Realise there are advantages for internal candidates . . .

Internal candidates have a variety of advantages during interviews, including:

✔ specific product (or service) knowledge that goes beyond that of candidates from similar roles in competing organisations

✔ relevant industry and client knowledge that should help them illustrate their answers with good examples from their experience

✔ a knowledge of office politics and particular company messages that will help them frame their answers within the context of the organisation

✔ better opportunities to research the advertised role—
they can make easier contact with previous job-holders,
or those with a stake in the new role

Step four: . . . as well as difficulties

As ever, there are downsides for internal candidates too.
They may find the interview process difficult because:

- they come across as too relaxed or overconfident
(which may be interpreted as arrogance) if they are
familiar with those interviewing them
- the interviewers may not be looking for 'more of the
same', which can be troublesome for internal
candidates who have been preparing to follow in their
boss's footsteps
- there's nowhere to hide. In interviews, candidates
often exaggerate their effectiveness in previous
roles, focusing strongly on positive performance
and forgetting to mention the bits that went badly
wrong. There is no chance that internal applicants
can get away with flannelling of this sort, so their
uninflated descriptions of performance may look
poor beside external candidates' rose-tinted
ones

Common mistakes

✗ You give internal interviews to new interviewers

An internal interview may seem to be less pressured than external ones—and therefore the ideal training ground for new interviewers—but in fact the opposite is true. The interviewer may find their existing relationship with, and knowledge of, the candidate difficult to put to one side. Communication around the interview, in making arrangements and giving feedback, is also more critical. Getting the tone wrong or handling sensitivities poorly are areas that new interviewers can find difficult at first; they may fear that the whole organisation will get to hear about any errors they make.

✗ You limit your vacancies

Don't rely on internal recruitment alone if you need to fill a post. If you don't advertise the position externally, you'll be limiting your chances of increasing the talent in your business. Clearly it's good to promote talent that is already in the business, as it helps you to retain and develop good employees, but only when they are shown to be the best candidate for the job.

✗ You ignore an unsuccessful internal candidate

Make new recruits feel welcome but don't ignore your existing members of staff, especially following an unsuccessful application. It's a sure-fire way to switch off a motivated employee. If an internal candidate is unsuccessful, give them clear feedback about why they were not the best person for the job on this occasion. By handling this carefully and putting it in the context of areas to work on and experience to gain, you can retain their skills and continue to develop them for your business.

STEPS TO SUCCESS

✔ To get the best result—that is, the right person for the job—treat internal candidates for a vacancy exactly as you treat external ones.

✔ If you're responsible for arranging an internal interview, make sure that the interview panel is impartial—positive bias can be just as damaging as negative. Apply the selection criteria fairly and consistently across all applicants to keep on safe ground.

✔ If your organisation is small or it's just impossible to find impartial interviewers, ask a neutral observer to attend. This could be someone from a different department or team, or even a trusted colleague from another organisation altogether.

✔ Remember that it's hard for internal candidates as well as for the interviewers; they do have some advantages, of course, but they also aren't able to create another 'good first impression' or seem like the best new thing

since sliced bread because you know them already.
Try to see it from both sides of the fence.

✔ Even though it seems like a natural step, don't 'break in'
first-time interviewers on internal candidates. As
discussed above, there are many potential pitfalls and
awkwardnesses to negotiate, so it's best to bring in your
most experienced interviewers wherever possible.

Useful link

Chartered Institute of Personnel and Development:
www.cipd.co.uk

Making a good selection decision

Now that the assessment stage is complete, you should have all the information you need to pick the right candidate. Yet even at this late stage, trained professionals can clutch failure from the jaws of victory and choose the wrong person. At this stage, there are still many pitfalls to avoid, so read on to find out how.

Step one: Understand the selection decision

The simplest selection decisions are where there are several candidates for one vacancy. Applicants are assessed on the attributes that are required for successful job performance by various methods including interviews. The possible outcomes are:

- a clear choice for the role is offered the job
- there is no clear choice but several candidates are considered and a choice made. The role is offered to this candidate
- there is no clear choice but several candidates are considered and a choice is made. The role

is offered to this candidate with a probationary
period
■ there is no clear choice and no candidates reach the
threshold to be considered. A choice is deferred until a
further round of advertising and assessment can be
completed

Obviously if there are several different vacancies the
decisions become more complex, as there are not only
decisions to be made about *whether* to take on each
candidate but also *how to deploy them* to cover all the
roles satisfactorily. This is often the case during graduate
selection 'milk-rounds'. Considering candidates in a 'parallel
process' for more than one role at a time is much less costly
than the 'serial' option. There would be little chance of
keeping candidates interested in the recruitment process
for several roles with separate assessments one after the
other. They'd soon be put off!

The risk of getting some decisions wrong rises with the
complexity. The cost of making wrong decisions either
with a 'false hit'—where you think you have found a
good candidate but she or he turns out to be a poor
performer on the job—or a 'false miss'—where you fail
to spot the best candidate and either hire the
second-best candidate or keep looking—could be very
high (see Chapter 1). So these decisions should not be
taken lightly.

Step two: Use your 'scorecard'

During the discussion stage, bring together all the assessment information in one 'scorecard'. Where you have more than one interviewer, make sure that the ratings given by each interviewer or observer are clear and supported by 'evidence' in the form of notes or test forms, if appropriate.

There are different ways to turn the information gathered into a prediction of how candidates will perform on the job, so that you can compare the candidates you have seen. But not all ways are equal. The reason that you need to be careful about how you do it is that errors creep in if you combine data using *judgment*. Judgment does play an important part in the selection process but that happens during assessments, interviews, and observations. Judgment is also required when placing a value on the package offered and is critical for negotiation.

When combination of the data on the scorecard is done using a formula that is **identical for each applicant** it is a *mechanical* process, which has been shown to improve the reliability of selection decisions, which means fewer expensive errors.

In large recruitment programmes, you will often have to collate lots of information to make your decision. Combining the data from interviews with work sample test results is a tricky area and how you do it can make a big difference. An HR expert should be involved at the design stage to ensure the correct (and most effective) method is used for the type of data you will be gathering.

All these methods assume that the selection decisions are continually being made, so that early in the process you can invest in improving the validity and reap the rewards later. If you are designing a process for a new, one-off, or infrequent vacancy, as often happens in small businesses, then you will need a simplified process.

A quick—but systematic—seven-step model

1 Identify the area of the role, the duties, tasks, and activities. What attributes will the successful applicant need to have?

2 Think of ways to find out about each attribute. For skills, perhaps you could ask applicants to perform a task like those in the role, while you observe and make a rating. For personal attributes, an interview and references may give the information you need.

3 Decide what weight the different areas rated should have, based on how important they are to the role.

4 Decide on any thresholds below which you will not consider the applicant. For example, let's say you are recruiting a driver. You must have someone with a clean driving licence, rather than someone who is about to take their test.

5 Use a rating sheet during the assessment stage with the applicants and make lots of notes. Ensure that

the process is the same for each candidate and that you rate on the criteria you decided on in advance. Guard against making decisions based on how similar the person is to you or whether you like them.

6 Remove any applicants that did not meet your thresholds.

7 Multiply each rating by the 'importance weighting' to give a weighted rating for that area. Add up the weighted ratings to give a total for each candidate.

Step three: Create your 'preferred' and your 'back-up' list

Your preferred candidate is, naturally, number one on the job performance prediction list. He or she is the best candidate for the job. Providing they meet the threshold critieria and have satisfactory references, he or she is your clear choice for the role.

Numbers two and three are back-ups, in case your first choice falls through. They should be contacted and told that they performed well and you will contact them again very soon with an answer.

Step four: Get in touch with those who didn't make it

Don't leave it too long before getting in touch with the people who definitely won't be offered a job with your organisation. Write a standard letter to each, thanking them for their time and their interest, stating the outcome of the process.

Try to add a personalised paragraph of feedback for each one, explaining why they have not been offered a role. If you made some brief feedback notes (as suggested in Chapter 3), then these paragraphs won't take long to put together and the candidates will find them very useful. Don't forget to wish them luck in finding their next role.

The letters that are harder to write are the ones for candidates who *did* meet the threshold level of job performance prediction but who are still not going to be offered a job. You want to be clear about the reasons for this, without suggesting that the candidates were inferior or that their skills were lacking.

For this group you need to explain that while they have the necessary requirements to perform the role, there were better candidates on the day. Encourage them to keep developing and add some appropriate, personalised feedback points.

For example:

> Dear Anne
>
> Thank you for attending interview for the sales role in our Bellbottom Branch. We regret to inform you that you have not been successful this time.
>
> The calibre of applicants was very high on the day, but as we only had one vacancy to fill we had to make a difficult decision based on the information that we gathered during our systematic interview process.
>
> While your interviewer rated you highly on trustworthiness and relevant job knowledge, she rated you as average for leadership skills and resilience. This was because you did not have many examples of projects where you have shown strengths in this area, and it was a specific criterion that we were looking for.
>
> This is, of course, something that you can develop with experience, so please do not be discouraged; we would consider another application from you in the future. We wish you all success with your current job search and wish you luck in your next role.
>
> Yours sincerely
>
> A N Other

Common mistakes

✗ You move the goalposts

Sometimes, after following a rigorous and systematic process, managers may decide that they don't like the candidate who has come out on top, so they give the role to someone else. Deciding to add extra criteria—such as likeability!—at the eleventh hour can invalidate the entire process. It also leaves you with no defence if a candidate decides to take action against you.

✗ You ignore the scorecard

If you give the job to anyone but the best candidate, you may be opening yourself up to legal action against you on grounds of *distributive* discrimination. Distributive justice means that all candidates have equal chances to apply and to succeed and should ensure that the best candidate gets the job.

STEPS TO SUCCESS

✔ Your well-designed, validated, systematic process is there to avoid poor selection decisions that can cost an organisation millions. Use it.

✔ When you (and your fellow interviewers, if appropriate) are ready to make your final selection choice, bring together all the assessment information and notes into one scorecard.

✓ As this can be a lengthy and tricky procedure, ask for advice from your company's HR department. If you run a small business, you could take advice from a freelance HR consultant or Business Link advisers.

✓ Work out who your preferred candidate is, and who would be your back-up choice.

✓ Get in touch promptly with those who didn't make either cut: thank them for their time, their interest in your business, and offer feedback on their performance.

✓ Avoid adding extra criteria at the last minute: all your careful work towards selecting the right person will be lost if you decide to add another hoop for them to jump through.

✓ Give the job to the best candidate.

Useful links

British Psychological Society:
www.bps.org.uk
Business Link:
www.businesslink.gov.uk

Making a job offer

The end is in sight! You've made your decision and know which candidate you want to hire for each vacancy. You need to offer a benefits package that will be attractive now and also motivating for some time to come. You'll also want to get a good deal for the organisation. Before you go any further, make sure that that the information on which you have based your decision is accurate.

Step one: Take up references

Some CVs look too good to be true . . . and some probably are! Applicants have been known to exaggerate, be economical with the truth, or even be extremely imaginative about their skills, knowledge, and attributes in order to get the job they want.

To make sure you're not taken for a ride, here are some recommendations:

✔ Make it clear in job advertisements and on application forms (if you're using them), that all candidates' references will be checked. Don't accept any applications without a reference.

✔ Ask for candidates' written permission to contact their references at an early stage, making sure that you have a named individual to talk to.

✔ When you speak to your contact, check at the very least that employment dates, salary or wage level (useful information for negotiation), position, and nature of the work carried out match what is stated on the CV or application form.

✔ Ask the contact if he or she worked closely with the candidate. If so, ask his or her opinion about the candidate's contribution.

✔ Make sure you are 'listening between the lines'. Information that is very brief, neutral, or given hesitantly suggests that something could be amiss. It is very rare that people will give a clearly negative reference—usually there is positive or neutral information.

✔ Ask for another reference if you're still not sure about offering the job to someone.

✔ If you *still* don't feel secure about the candidate's past performance, don't hire them.

Employers are not required to give references for their past employees, except for a few posts in the financial services sector. Any references that you receive must be treated as confidential but be aware of obligations under the Data Protection Act. People can ask to see their personnel file and other information that you hold about them, including references from a previous employer if you have kept them. You may be required legally to reveal to an individual all this information.

There are instances—for example, for new health workers— where employers need to collect health information about the people they recruit. Do not ask for medical information until it is required and only where you need the information to be sure that the person is fit to carry out the role. It's extremely important that you keep this information secure and confidential.

Step two: Think about the 'psychological contract'

Remember that what goes into an employment contract is not only tangible elements—usually the employee's time and effort in return for the organisation's money— but also psychological elements. Jobs are not expected to last for life any more, so smart employees are looking for other rewards to compensate for lack of job security. These recent changes mean that applicants have become more clued up about the 'psychological contract'.

At interview, candidates start to build up an impression of the way that the organisation operates. They may have met their future colleagues and formed a view about how well they'll fit into the culture.

You'll have asked questions that gave you a view of what makes them tick and this will help you work out which elements of a psychological contract will be important for *them*. A very attractive job offer is one that is tailored to the individual and clarifies how their needs will be met. It also sets out the values of the organisation and the expectations the employer has of its employees.

Step three: Make a job offer by phone

There are five main advantages to starting the offer process using the telephone:

1 you can convey your enthusiasm about the role in what you say, and how you say it

2 you can give the successful candidate some really positive feedback about why you have chosen them

3 you can start the negotiation by outlining the benefits package

4 you can gauge the successful applicant's reaction to the package and make changes—if necessary—before sending out the written offer letter, making it more likely that the written offer will be accepted

5 where time is of the essence, you can get immediate feedback, which will make negotiation quicker

When you get in touch with a successful applicant, start the conversation by congratulating him or her on getting the job. Try to get across your own positive feelings about the final selection and if you feel it's appropriate, why he or she was the best candidate.

Say that you'll be confirming the offer in writing, then outline the role, especially any areas that were sketchy at the interview stage, or where the role's boundaries have changed to reflect the skills of the individual recruited. Outline the benefits package to them, explaining the basic rate of pay and any bonuses, if appropriate. Depending on the type of job offered, you could also explain what the typical career path is from this role in the future, if applicable. Answer any questions, making sure that you're as accurate as you can be, since discrepancies between phone and written offers may make the candidate nervous. If you can't answer a question there and then, it's much better to say that you'll investigate and get back to the successful candidate than to make something up and have to retract it later.

Finally, ask the candidate for his or her initial reaction. Know which items in the package are 'core', and unlikely to change, and which could be changed if necessary. Listen carefully to any concerns: is it the tangible or the psychological items that the candidate is concerned about? What does he or she like about the offer?

Step four: Compose a written job offer

It's usual to send two signed copies of the offer letter to the successful applicant and ask them to confirm his or her acceptance by signing both copies and sending one back to you. Here are the elements that you need to address in a written job offer:

✔ the name of the successful candidate

✔ the name of the position and a short description of the role and who he or she will be reporting to

✔ the nature of the role: contract or permanent, full or part time

✔ the start date and the length of any probationary period

✔ the number of hours per week and the timing of those hours, where necessary

✔ number of holidays

✔ the terms you are offering: wage rate or salary per annum, whether this is performance linked or not, benefits such as pension or health cover and any bonuses that are offered

✔ any training and development that candidates will be expected to complete, and the timing of these

State clearly how the candidate should confirm his or her acceptance of the offer and give a deadline too. It's worth making clear that if references and other checks are unsatisfactory, the offer may be withdrawn or the probationary period may be longer.

You also need to ask them for evidence of their right to work in the United Kingdom. For most new recruits, this will be a document that bears their National Insurance number, such as:

- National Insurance number card
- a letter from a government agency
- a P45
- a pay slip
- a P60 form

Other documents can be used, but you need to check with the Home Office for up-to-date details of these.

Common mistakes

✗ You don't move quickly enough

Great candidates will be sought out and spotted by other employers too. When you come across real talent, act quickly and make an attractive offer if you want to get that person working for you. Keep things moving and make sure you make the necessary checks as quickly as you can.

✗ You discriminate 'accidentally'

When you're trying to find out if someone is suitable for a particular role, look for the information that you need and that *only*. For example, if you turn down candidates on the basis of health records that are *not* relevant to the role then candidates may be able to claim disability discrimination. This can also be the case with other checks that you run, such as on criminal records.

You mustn't offer less favourable contractual terms (including pay and benefits) to people because of their disability, gender/sexual orientation, religion, race, or because they are working part-time. Doing so could lead to a complaint of discrimination against you.

STEPS TO SUCCESS

✔ Be sure to check the accuracy of any information you're given by candidates: don't just assume it's correct.

✔ Don't be afraid to ask for a reference: every candidate should be able to give you one. Even candidates coming straight from school or college should be able to get a character reference from their tutor or a friend of the family.

✔ Make sure that you have a candidate's permission to approach their referees in relation to the role. Permission in writing is best.

✔ When you are putting together a job offer, think about the psychological elements of the contract as well as the tangible elements.

✔ Contact successful candidates by phone first, making

sure that you come across as positive and enthusiastic about the role.

✓ Listen carefully to their feedback and adjust your offer if necessary.

✓ Don't forget to ask for evidence that they are eligible to work in the UK.

✓ Send the prospective employee two copies of the job offer so that they can sign both, return one to you and keep the other for their records.

Useful links

Business Link:
www.businesslink.gov.uk
Experian offers a service to check higher education qualifications:
www.cvverifier.com/cv/cvmenu.shtml#reports
The Home Office:
www.homeoffice.gov.uk/equality-diversity
National Academic Recognition Information Centre (NARIC):
www.naric.org.uk
The Learning and Skills Council:
www.lsc.gov.uk/selectlsc.asp?sectio=/Corporate
The Criminal Records Bureau (CRB):
www.crb.gov.uk

Where to find more help

Competency-based Recruitment and Selection: A Practical Guide
Robert Wood, Tim Payne
Chichester: Wiley, 1998
214pp ISBN: 0471974730

Based on professional research, this book provides a comprehensive overview to best practice in recruitment and selection. It offers a practical, step-by-step approach that all HR professionals would benefit from.

The Definitive Book of Body Language: How to Read Others' Attitudes by Their Gestures
Allan Pease, Barbara Pease
London: Orion, 2005
400pp ISBN: 0752858785

Although asking the right questions is the main key to a successful interview, being able to interpret other people's body language will give you a great insight into what they *really* feel about something or someone. This book claims to help you 'learn to read other people's thoughts by their gestures'. Once you know the basics, you'll be able to use this knowledge to your advantage in interviews and, in fact, in all type of occasions.

Recruitment (Teach Yourself series)
Edward Peppitt
London: Teach Yourself, 2003
192pp ISBN: 0340799897
This short, focused book guides managers through the whole process of recruitment and selection. Its size and accessibility mean that it is useful for all managers, not just those with a background in HR.